I CAN BE...

I CAN BE SPORTY

AMAZING ATHLETES
WHO PUSHED THE BOUNDARIES

BY SHALINI VALLEPUR

Enslow PUBLISHING

Published in 2021 by Enslow Publishing, LLC
101 W. 23rd Street, Suite 240,
New York, NY 10011

© 2020 Booklife Publishing
This edition is published by arrangement with Booklife Publishing

Cataloging-in-Publication Data

Names: Vallepur, Shalinli.
Title: I can be sporty: amazing athletes who pushed the boundaries / Shalini Vallepur.
Description: New York : Enslow Publishing, 2021. | Series: I can be... | Includes glossary and index.
Identifiers: ISBN 9781978519718 (pbk.) | ISBN 9781978519732 (library bound) | ISBN 9781978519725 (6 pack)
Subjects: LCSH: Athletes--Biography--Juvenile literature. | Olympic athletes--Biography--Juvenile literature. | Sports--History--Juvenile literature.
Classification: LCC GV697.A1 V35 2020 | DDC 796.092'2 B--dc23

Printed in the United States of America

CPSIA compliance information: Batch #BS20ENS: For further information contact Enslow Publishing, New York, New York at 1-800-542-2595

IMAGE CREDITS

All images are courtesy of Shutterstock.com, unless otherwise specified. With thanks to Getty Images, Thinkstock Photo and iStockphoto.
Cover and throughout – asantosg, Forest Foxy, WINS86. 6 – primiaou. 7 – Sue Robinson. 8 – Shamanska Kate. 9 – Have a nice day Photo.
12 – Natasha Pankina. 13 – PiLart. 14 – primiaou, schab. 15 – akkachai thothubthai. 16 – ALEXHIIV. 17 – Macrovector. 19 – Brian A Jackson,
Ket4up. 21 – Ruslan Kim Studio, KIRIMARA. 22 – Natasha Pankina. 23 – Alhovik. 24 – was a. 25 – sportpoinT, Stock Vector. 27 – vectorplus,
Fred Ho. 29 – Vova_31. 30 – fullvector.

CONTENTS

PAGE 4 .... I Can Be...Sporty

PAGE 6 .... Gertrude Ederle

PAGE 8 .... Jesse Owens

PAGE 10 .... Be Like Owens

PAGE 12 .... Pelé

PAGE 14 .... Bruce Lee

PAGE 16 .... Muhammad Ali

PAGE 18 .... Jackie Joyner-Kersee

PAGE 20 .... Be Like Joyner-Kersee

PAGE 22 .... Serena Williams

PAGE 24 .... Usain Bolt

PAGE 26 .... Geeta Phogat

PAGE 28 .... Ellie Simmonds

PAGE 30 .... Medals and More

PAGE 31 .... Glossary

PAGE 32 .... Index

WORDS THAT LOOK LIKE this CAN BE FOUND IN THE GLOSSARY ON PAGE 31.

i CAN BE...
SPORTY

Have you ever been to see a soccer game? Or watched a tennis match on TV? Sporty people all over the world spend their lives training to compete in competitions such as the Olympic Games. But why do we compete and play sports?

People have always pushed themselves to be good at certain things, and sports are no different.

Sports can be hard, but they are also a good way to overcome many problems. There is a sport for everyone. It doesn't matter where somebody comes from or if they have a disability.

Read on to learn about the lives of some super sporty people who have shown the world the amazing things people can do.

GERTRUDE EDERLE

Born: 1905 Died: 2003

Gertrude Ederle was brought up in New York City. Ederle caught <u>measles</u> when she was five years old and started to lose hearing in one ear. However, this didn't hold her back. She began swimming and, when she was a teenager, she trained as a competitive swimmer.

Ederle found huge success in <u>long-distance</u> swimming. She started competing in bigger and bigger competitions and went on to win medals in the 1924 Olympic Games. After winning many competitions, Ederle set her sights on something even more challenging: swimming the English Channel. At the time, only five men had swum the 21 miles (33 km) across the English Channel. Ederle wanted to be the first woman to swim the dangerous and tough journey.

After being blown off course during her first attempt and having to be taken out of the water, she succeeded on her second attempt. She was again blown off course the second time, which meant she swam a massive 35 miles (56 km). However, she had still beaten the previous record set by men by more than two hours. Everybody celebrated Ederle's amazing achievement.

Ederle continued swimming, but soon her hearing problems got worse. She became a swimming teacher and helped deaf children learn to swim.

"TO ME, THE SEA IS LIKE A PERSON...WHEN I
SWIM IN THE SEA, I TALK TO IT.
I NEVER FEEL ALONE WHEN I'M OUT THERE."
- GERTRUDE EDERLE

JESSE OWENS

Born: 1913 Died: 1980

James Owens grew up in Ohio. He was the youngest of ten children. His grandfather had been a <u>slave</u>, and his father worked as a farmer. Growing up, Owens helped his father in the fields. Owens was given the nickname Jesse by a schoolteacher, and it stuck.

A high school <u>coach</u> noticed how fast Owens could run and encouraged him to start training. Owens began to set new records in athletics in his school and in Ohio. He became the captain of the college athletics team. However, because of <u>racial segregation</u> in the United States, he was not allowed to live at college or eat with the white team members. Despite this, Owens kept smashing records and winning races.

Owens went on to compete in the 1936 Olympics in Berlin, Germany, the first Olympic Games to be shown on TV. These games happened while <u>Nazi</u> leader Adolf Hitler was in power in Berlin. Hitler's views were <u>racist</u>. He thought that white people were better than others, and he thought they would do better at the Olympics. Owens proved Hitler wrong when he won four gold medals.

When Owens returned to the United States, he was not congratulated by the president, which was something the president did for many other athletes. Despite this, Owens' great achievements were not forgotten, and he spent the rest of his life training new athletes.

"IF I COULD JUST WIN THOSE GOLD MEDALS, I SAID TO MYSELF, THE HITLERS OF THE WORLD WOULD HAVE NO MORE MEANING FOR ME. FOR ANYONE, MAYBE."
- JESSE OWENS

BE LIKE OWENS AND PROVE PEOPLE WRONG.

BE LIKE OWENS

MAKE A MEDAL

Owens won many medals during his career.
Medals are used to reward athletes for their achievements.
Let's make a medal!

YOU WILL NEED:

A jar lid

Cardboard

Pens and pencils

Ribbon

Gold glitter

Scissors

PVA glue

Get an adult to help you with the scissors!

1. Draw a star or any other shape on the cardboard and cut it out. Make sure it can fit onto the jar lid.

2. Glue the shape onto the jar lid.

3. Cover the jar lid in a thin layer of glue.

4. Sprinkle the glitter all over the jar lid and leave it to dry completely.

5. Make a loop with the ribbon, and glue it to the back of the jar lid so you can wear the medal.

6. Wear your medal – you're a winner!

Why not make medals for your friends and family? You could write "Funniest Friend" or "Amazing Aunt" and give them out as awards.

PELÉ

Born: 1940

Edson Arantes do Nascimento was born in Brazil. His family didn't have a lot of money. Nascimento played soccer in the streets with a sock stuffed with rags. Nascimento's friends gave him the nickname "Pelé" and it stuck. Pelé joined a youth team, and his soccer skills got better and better. He was picked to play with a **professional** soccer club as a goal scorer when he was only 15 years old.

Pelé became a **national** hero in Brazil, and it wasn't long before he joined the Brazilian national team. He played in the 1958 World Cup when he was only 17 years old. He stunned the world with his talent on the soccer field, scoring many goals and helping Brazil win the World Cup.

Many European soccer clubs wanted Pelé to play for their team, but Pelé stayed in Brazil. He went on to help Brazil win two more World Cups. Pelé became a huge soccer star around the world, and he also did a lot of work to help others. Pelé understood what it was like to have a difficult childhood, so he worked with charities to help children.

"SUCCESS IS NO ACCIDENT. IT IS HARD WORK, PERSEVERANCE, LEARNING, STUDYING, SACRIFICE, AND MOST OF ALL, LOVE OF WHAT YOU ARE DOING OR LEARNING TO DO."
- PELÉ

BE LIKE PELÉ AND ALWAYS WORK HARD.

BRUCE LEE

Born: 1940 Died: 1973

Lee Jun Fan was born in an American hospital and was given the name "Bruce" by one of the nurses. Lee left the United States and grew up in Hong Kong. He was interested in many different things growing up, such as dance and poetry. He even appeared in films as a child actor. Lee got into trouble with <u>gangs</u> as a teenager. He began to learn a style of <u>martial arts</u> called <u>kung fu</u> so that he could protect himself. He was extremely talented at kung fu.

Lee moved back to the United States when he was 18 years old. He went to college and supported himself by teaching kung fu. He created his own style of martial arts called jeet kune do. Lee was spotted by somebody in the film industry while giving a demonstration. He started to act again and starred in TV shows and films. His fourth film was the first martial arts film to be made by a Hollywood studio. Lee had lots of success with films, but he never stopped teaching and passing on his skills. He taught kung fu to many celebrities too. He was dedicated to his sport and had an extremely strict training plan.

Lee passed away when he was only 32. He helped bring Asian culture to the United States and inspired people around the world to take part in martial arts.

BE LIKE LEE AND AIM HIGH.

"DON'T FEAR FAILURE. NOT FAILURE, BUT LOW AIM, IS THE CRIME. IN GREAT ATTEMPTS, IT IS GLORIOUS EVEN TO FAIL."
- BRUCE LEE

MUHAMMAD ALI

Born: 1942 Died: 2016

Cassius Clay, Jr. was born in Kentucky. Growing up there in that time was hard because of racial segregation. Clay, his family, and other black Americans weren't allowed to go to the same places as white Americans. When Clay was 12, somebody stole his bike. Clay told the police officer that he wanted to fight the person who stole his bike. The police officer was a boxing coach and offered to teach Clay how to box, taking his fighting away from the streets and into a boxing ring.

Clay competed in <u>amateur</u> boxing matches. He fought over 100 matches and won more than 90 of them. His life changed when he competed in the 1960 Olympic Games and won a gold medal. He decided to start competing professionally. Clay became the <u>heavyweight</u> champion of the world and a famous celebrity. He was known for his new and different style of boxing and his confidence inside and outside the boxing ring.

In 1964, Clay began to follow the religion of Islam and changed his name to Muhammad Ali. He <u>retired</u> from boxing in 1981 and used his fame to improve life for black Americans as well as promote world peace. He is remembered as one of the greatest boxers of all time.

"IF MY MIND CAN CONCEIVE IT
AND MY HEART CAN BELIEVE IT,
THEN I CAN ACHIEVE IT."
- MUHAMMAD ALI

BE LIKE ALI AND
PUSH YOURSELF TO BE THE BEST.

JACKIE JOYNER-KERSEE

Born: 1962

Jacqueline Joyner grew up in Illinois. She was a sporty child and never said no to trying new sports. Joyner joined her school's sports teams and competed in volleyball and basketball. Joyner did well in these sports and was given a basketball <u>scholarship</u> to go to college.

Joyner started training to compete in the <u>heptathlon</u>. At this time, the heptathlon wasn't a popular event. However, Joyner brought attention to it at the Olympic Games and other worldwide competitions by winning medals. In 1983, Joyner was told she had <u>asthma</u>. She struggled with the condition as it had an effect on her competitive skills. She tried her best to win the gold medal in the heptathlon at the 1984 Olympic Games, but missed out by a few points. This made her more determined to win gold at the next Olympic Games. In 1986, Joyner married her coach, Bob Kersee, and changed her name to Joyner-Kersee.

After years of hard work and training, Joyner-Kersee won the gold medal for the heptathlon at the 1988 Olympic Games. She also set a new world record and scored more points than any other woman. She saw more success at the 1992 Olympic Games when she won gold again. She was given the Jesse Owens Award for her achievements in sports, and, in 2013, the Jackie Joyner-Kersee Award was established. Joyner-Kersee's story has inspired people to overcome their conditions and to never give up.

BE LIKE JOYNER-KERSEE AND NEVER STOP TRAINING TO BE THE BEST YOU CAN BE.

"THE ONLY PERSON WHO CAN STOP YOU FROM REACHING YOUR GOALS IS YOU."
- JACKIE JOYNER-KERSEE

BE LIKE JOYNER-KERSEE

THE HEPTATHLON

Have you ever watched a heptathlon or competed in one?
Let's take a look at the seven different events in a heptathlon, and recreate one!

1) 100-meter hurdles: Athletes run and jump over ten hurdles over a distance of 100 meters (328 feet).

2) High jump: Athletes have a short run of 15 meters (49 feet) before launching themselves over a bar.

3) Shot put: Using a special spinning movement, athletes throw an iron ball as far as they can.

4) 200 m run: Athletes race against each other over 200 meters (656 feet).

5) Running long jump: Athletes run about 30 meters (98 feet), then jump forward into a pit of sand.

6) Javelin throw: Athletes run a short distance and throw a javelin as far as they can.

7) 800 m run: Athletes race against each other over 800 m (0.5 mile).

BEAN BAG SHOT PUT

YOU WILL NEED:

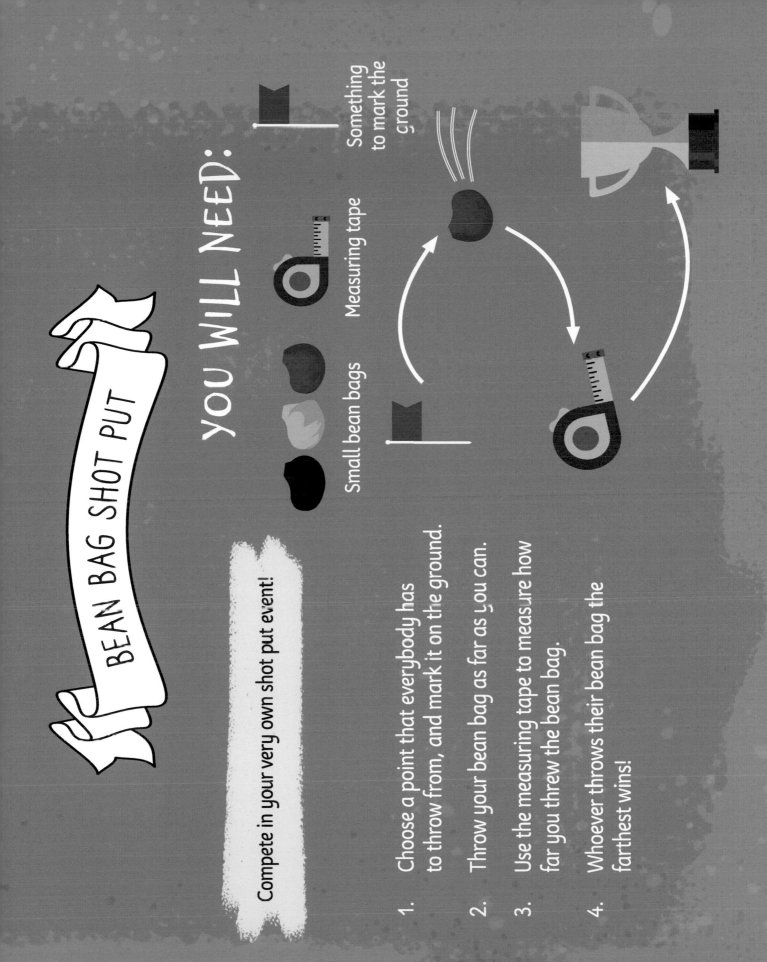

Something to mark the ground

Measuring tape

Small bean bags

Compete in your very own shot put event!

1. Choose a point that everybody has to throw from, and mark it on the ground.

2. Throw your bean bag as far as you can.

3. Use the measuring tape to measure how far you threw the bean bag.

4. Whoever throws their bean bag the farthest wins!

SERENA WILLIAMS

Born: 1981

Serena Williams grew up with four sisters and her parents in Compton, California. Serena started playing tennis with her older sister Venus when she was three years old. Williams won her first tournament when she was only four years old.

Serena turned professional when she was 14 years old, a year after Venus turned professional. Both sisters had their own style of playing that impressed audiences everywhere. They teamed up to compete in doubles tournaments, and together they have gone on to win 14 <u>Grand Slam</u> doubles titles! By the end of 2019, Williams had won 23 Grand Slam singles titles as well as four gold medals in the Olympic Games. But this didn't come easily.

Williams has faced many challenges along the way. Along with injuries, Williams has dealt with many obstacles within the tennis world and criticism for things such as the clothes she wears. But these challenges and setbacks didn't stop her from becoming one of the greatest tennis players in history.

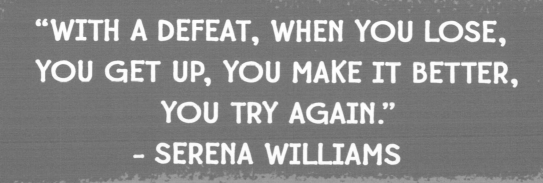

BE LIKE WILLIAMS AND PICK YOURSELF UP WHEN YOU FALL DOWN.

"WITH A DEFEAT, WHEN YOU LOSE, YOU GET UP, YOU MAKE IT BETTER, YOU TRY AGAIN."
- SERENA WILLIAMS

USAIN BOLT

Born: 1986

Growing up in Jamaica, Usain Bolt loved playing soccer and cricket. One day, his cricket coach noticed how fast he could <u>sprint</u>. The coach believed that Bolt would be an amazing runner and convinced him to start training. Bolt was a huge success in school and local competitions. He won a gold medal in the 2002 World Junior Championships, becoming the youngest ever world junior champion in any event.

Bolt injured his <u>hamstring</u> before competing in the 2004 Olympic Games. It was a major setback, and he failed to win any medals. Bolt didn't give up and trained harder than ever. He competed in the 2008 Olympic Games and won three gold medals as well as beat previous world records. Although the hamstring injury got better after a while, Bolt has a long-term condition called <u>scoliosis</u>. He had to work hard to make sure his injuries and scoliosis didn't slow him down.

Bolt became a famous star around the world. He has set up his own charity that promotes education for children so that everybody can achieve their dreams.

"ANYTHING IS POSSIBLE;
I DON'T THINK LIMITS."
- USAIN BOLT

BOLT

BE LIKE BOLT AND PUSH YOURSELF.

GEETA PHOGAT

Born: 1988

Geeta Phogat was born in a small village in India. Her father was a wrestler. He wanted to have a son whom he could teach to wrestle, but instead he had four daughters. It was normal in Phogat's village for girls to stay at home and get married when they were young. Phogat's father wanted something different for his daughters so he decided to train them in wrestling.

Many people in the village gossiped about Phogat and her family. They thought girls shouldn't be allowed to wrestle. Phogat didn't listen to them. She followed her father's strict training, and she began to compete in wrestling competitions in India. She even cut her hair off so that it wouldn't get in the way when she practiced.

Phogat competed in the 2010 Commonwealth Games. She won a gold medal and brought wrestling to India's attention. In 2012, she became the first Indian woman to compete as a wrestler in the Olympic Games. By the end of 2018, Phogat had won a gold medal in the Commonwealth Games, two gold medals in the Commonwealth Championships, and a gold medal in the Asian Olympic Qualification Tournament. Phogat has inspired other girls in India to take up wrestling.

"IT'S ABOUT HARD WORK AND NOT GENDER."
– GEETA PHOGAT

BE LIKE PHOGAT AND DON'T LET OTHER PEOPLE STOP YOU FROM DOING WHAT YOU LOVE.

ELLIE SIMMONDS

Born: 1994

Eleanor Simmonds was born in Great Britain with achondroplasia. Achondroplasia is a condition that means a person's legs and arms do not grow to their full length and are short compared with the person's <u>torso</u>. Simmonds started swimming when she was five years old. She was very competitive when she was a child and liked to win when playing board games and in races at school. She became interested in taking swimming more seriously and training harder after she saw the 2004 Paralympic Games on TV.

When Simmonds was 13 years old, she competed in the 2008 Paralympic Games. She was the youngest person to compete for Great Britain that year, and she surprised everybody when she won two gold medals. Simmonds shows no signs of slowing down. She has won many more gold medals in major competitions.

Simmonds makes swimming look easy, but she faced many challenges along the way. She had an operation on her legs when she was 12 years old, and she had to move away from her family so that she could train properly. Simmonds was <u>appointed</u> an <u>OBE</u> when she was 18 years old to celebrate her hard work and achievements in the Paralympics.

BE LIKE SIMMONDS AND DO EVERYTHING THAT YOU WANT TO DO.

"IM A NORMAL PERSON, JUST A LOT SMALLER. I GET ON WITH IT. EVERYBODY SHOULD DO THAT....GO OUT AND ACHIEVE WHATEVER YOU WANT."
- ELLIE SIMMONDS

MEDALS AND MORE

Take a look at just a few of the achievements and **accolades** achieved by the sporty people in this book.

GERTRUDE EDERLE — QUEEN OF THE WAVES

First woman to swim across the English Channel

JESSE OWENS — BUCKEYE BULLET

Three-time Olympic gold medalist

PELÉ — THE BLACK PEARL

2000 FIFA Football Player of the Century

MUHAMMAD ALI — THE GREATEST

World Heavyweight Champion 1964–67, 1974–78, 1978–79

BRUCE LEE — LITTLE PHOENIX

Founder of Jeet Kune Do

JACKIE JOYNER-KERSEE

Three-time Olympic gold medalist

SERENA WILLIAMS

23-time Grand Slam singles champion

USAIN BOLT — LIGHTNING BOLT

100 m world record holder – 9.58 seconds

GEETA PHOGAT

First female Indian wrestler at the Olympic Games

ELLIE SIMMONDS

Two-time Paralympic gold medalist and youngest person to be appointed an **MBE**

GLOSSARY

accolades	marks of approval or awards
amateur	someone who does something for fun rather than professionally
appointed	to be given a job or a title
asthma	a condition that affects the lungs
coach	a person who trains athletes
gangs	groups of people who sometimes commit crimes
Grand Slam	the four most important annual tennis events
hamstring	a muscle that is at the back of a person's leg, between the hip and the knee
heavyweight	a category of boxers who weigh above a certain amount
heptathlon	a sporting event that is made up of seven different events
javelin	a spear-like pole that is used in some sports
kung fu	a type of martial art that comes from China
long-distance	traveling a long way
martial arts	a group of sports that use the body to defend and attack
MBE	MBE stands for Member of the British Empire; an award given for an outstanding achievement or service to the community
measles	a disease that causes fever and a red skin rash
national	relating to a nation
Nazi	a political party that controlled Germany from 1933 to 1945 and fought in World War II
OBE	OBE stands for Officer of the Most Excellent Order of the British Empire; an award given for outstanding achievements in a person's chosen area
professional	someone who does a job that needs special training
racial segregation	separating people based on their race
racist	treating somebody badly or unfairly because of their race
retired	to have stopped working professionally
scholarship	money that is given to students to help them pay for school or college
scoliosis	when a person's spine is slightly curved
slave	a person who has no freedom and is owned by another person
sprint	a short, fast run
torso	the body from the neck to the hips

INDEX

A

athletes 8–10, 18–20, 24–25, 30
athletics 8, 18, 20–21, 24

B

boxing 16–17

C

coaches 8–9, 16, 18, 24
Commonwealth Games 26

E

English Channel 6, 30

F

families 11–12, 16, 26, 28

H

heptathlon 18–21

I

injuries 22, 24

K

kung fu 14–15

M

medals 6–11, 16–19, 22–30

O

Olympic Games 4, 6, 8, 16, 18, 22, 24, 26, 30

P

Paralympics 28, 30

S

soccer 4, 12–13, 24, 30
swimming 6–7, 28–30

T

tennis 4, 22–23
throwing 20–21
tournaments 12–13, 22, 26
training 4, 6, 8, 14, 18–19, 24, 26, 28

W

wrestling 26–27